JESUS AND DIRT

A Fresh Look at

The Parable of the Sower

Michael D. Stover

JESUS AND DIRT - A Fresh Look at the Parable of the Sower

Copyright © 2016 by Michael D. Stover

All rights reserved. No part of this book may be reproduced or transmitted in any form or by any means without written permission from the author.

Printed in USA

First Printing, 2016

ISBN-13: 978-1541207073

ISBN-10: 1541207076

Unless otherwise indicated, all Scripture quotations are taken from the Holy Bible, New Living Translation, copyright © 1996, 2004, 2007, 2013, 2015 by Tyndale House Foundation. Used by permission of Tyndale House Publishers, Inc., Carol Stream, Illinois 60188. All rights reserved.

Scripture quotations marked HCSB®, are taken from the Holman Christian Standard Bible®, Copyright © 1999, 2000, 2002, 2003, 2009 by Holman Bible Publishers. Used by permission. HCSB® is a federally registered trademark of Holman Bible Publishers.

Table of Contents

Foreword	v
Introduction	vii
Chapter 1 - Path Ground	1
Chapter 2 - Stony Ground	10
Chapter 3 - Thorny Ground	15
Chapter 4 - Good Ground	22
Chapter 5 - Dull Hearts	26
Summary	29
About the Author	31
Also by the Author	32
Appendix	34

Foreword

The parable of the soils is one of those teachings of Jesus that has become so well known it is like an old pair of slippers, or the pathway home from work. It's just something we take for granted; we assume we know what it means. In our journey as a follower of Christ, we assume that we have mined it for all the spiritual truth that can be found. I daresay there will be few followers of Christ that will be exposed to the parable for the first time in this book. In the church world, preaching and teaching on the parable of the soils is as common as - well, as common as DIRT!

So, why in the world would any writer add to the volumes that have already been penned about this subject, and why should you bother to read it? The answer is simple. Michael Stover lifts this teaching from the pages of Scripture and weaves it gently into the fabric of our lives. As he discusses each type of soil that Jesus mentions, readers can see themselves and the condition of their own soil.

I found myself reliving my own conversion experience and considering what the soil must have been like in my young, nine-year-old heart as God worked His amazing work of redemption. It made me think of seasons in my life when the Word that was intended to grow me into a strong, life-giving plant in the Kingdom was choked out by the thorns and weeds of life and bad choices. It made me pause to reflect and rejoice over those supernatural moments when the Master Gardener sowed

His good seed into the soil of my heart. Moments when it was perfectly tilled and prepared for just what He was accomplishing in me.

Michael has been good enough to include some preaching/teaching outlines in this book for you to use. But, don't get so caught up in it as a resource for being a professional Christ-follower that you fail to see your own dirt. Take time to remember your own encounters with God, and consider how your soil and its condition have affected your journey with Christ. If necessary, get out the spiritual tiller or hoe and get to work. You have got a lot of growing left to do, and that soil needs to be ready for what is coming next!

Pastor Pete Tackett
Antioch Baptist Church
Johnson City, TN
http://www.petetackett.com
Author of re.VITAL.ize: Lessons Learned in a Recovering Church

Introduction

Jesus was an amalgamation of profundity and simplicity. God and human. Redeemer become servant. Creator and carpenter. Lord and sacrificial lamb. Because He was God he spoke with authority, and His words still resonate today. Because he was a simple Jewish carpenter, accustomed to a common life, He spoke with simplicity - and His words still resonate today. My proof? This book, and others like it, seeks to reexamine His words and reapply them to new audiences. People and societies change: Jesus' words still engage and transform. Rich man, poor man, beggar man, thief; doctor, lawyer, Indian chief. All are still profoundly affected by the words of God, the simple carpenter. Jesus was an amalgamation of profundity and simplicity.

This parable is a fine example of my assertion concerning Jesus' simplicity and profundity. He chose to speak in simple stories that engaged the common people, stories about fishing and food, pearls and pigs... and dirt. This parable should really be entitled "The Parable of the Soil", because the story, and the truths emphasized therein, do not focus on the one sowing seed. The sower is doing what sowers do: scattering seed on the ground in order to gain a harvest. Is the sower important? Vastly so, for without a sower no seed would be shared, and therefore, no harvest would be reaped. But that is a topic for another volume.

The focus of the story is about the soil. It's about dirt. In Matthew 13, Jesus taught how the hearts of people can differ regarding openness, or receptiveness, to God's Word. And who knows the hearts of mankind better than the Creator/Carpenter? He has the dirt on all of us! His analogy uses dirt in various conditions to represent each type of person. This is not a book of new discoveries. It's a reexamination of simple, yet profound, truths as only Jesus could share them. We tend to forget those truths. Or, we choose to forget. Both categories of people are addressed in Jesus' parable. So, if you have heard, yet forgotten, follow along as we play in the dirt with Jesus. If you've never played in the dirt with Jesus through this parable, I dare you to take simple pleasure in, and plumb the exacting depths of....dirt.

Chapter 1 – Path Ground
Matthew 13:1-9, 18-19

Life happens. One day at a time. It's the same for all of us. No one is immune, no one gets extra time, no one gets their days in advance. We all grind along at the same pace. I'm convinced most people wander away from the faith one slow day at a time. There are cataclysmic shifts in churches that do untold damage, driving scores away from the church and the faith. There will be more. But I still believe the daily grind of living by faith, of choosing to *live out* our faith, wears away more people than church explosions blast away.

I have no research to prove my thesis. I have no data charts to bedazzle info-mongers; no statistics to quote that others will forget. I only have my convictions formed from years in the local church. And, of course, Jesus' Parable of the Sower.

I remember when I was a small boy my parents would sometimes talk in code to hide their conversation. This especially happened at Christmas, when they were making plans for gifts, but didn't want nosy little ears to overhear. Their conversation was for those ready to hear; it wasn't time to reveal my Christmas gifts. I was excluded, on purpose, from the conversation.

Jesus embraced similar logic when He used parables in His teaching. There were always crowds straining to hear His words. But some of those words were not for everyone in the crowd. Some were not ready to receive them; others were. So,

Jesus told stories to communicate His truths to those ready to hear.

In the Parable of the Sower, Jesus uses the simplest of analogies to communicate immense Kingdom truths: farming. Israel in Jesus' day was primarily an agrarian society and many could identify with, if not understand, the word pictures He employed. After reading His parable in Matthew 13:1-9, and the explanation given in verses 18-23, the basics of the story are clear:

A Simple Explanation of the Analogy

- The Seed - Word of God

- The Sower – Jesus (and by extension, those who share God's Word with others)

- The Soil – The hearts of men and women, with different levels of receptivity

Everyone's heart condition is represented by the types of soil in Jesus' parable. You could say Jesus has the dirt on everyone!

Unprepared Ground

Imagine a neatly cultivated field. In our day such work is performed by machines, and productivity demands that every square foot of acreage be used. No so in Jesus' day. Tilling the ground was accomplished by hand, and paths allowed farmers and travelers, and their pack animals, to traverse between fields. This ground grew hard through ceaseless walking. The alternating cold and heat of the seasons further tempered these undisturbed paths. This is what Jesus referred to as 'the path'.

Such ground was unprepared for seed. No prior efforts or preparations were made to make the soil ready to receive seed. Therefore, when seed fell upon this hardened soil, it simply bounced around and lay naked in the sunshine. And lying in the open it became ready sustenance for every passing bird.

This path ground is a word picture for men and women whose hearts have been hardened by exposure to negative elements. Trodden down by the harsh realities of life. Pummeled by coarse interactions with people. Baked and scorched by the hot, searing effects of willful disobedience. Our culture glorifies everything that Scripture opposes. We are bombarded with messages encouraging us to "get what's coming to us" by any means necessary. We glorify those who "get ahead" and ignore the lines they crossed and the people they crushed.

When our efforts at sharing the Good News meet with no response it's because the ground is unprepared. There's been little or no exposure to God's Word. His Spirit is clearly not working to soften up the heart and give understanding. The person may have had no exposure to spiritual things, or repeated exposure to worldly religious dogmas until they are hardened toward anything that smacks of the spiritual.

I remember conversations with people in my early years of ministry when I discovered they had never been told about Jesus. It simply astounded me to grasp that people in the "buckle of the Bible belt" areas of our country had never before been explained the story of the gospel. And even when it was explained, their response was some variation of "so what?"

One time in particular I visited with a family in a large hospital in Memphis, Tennessee who were waiting patiently as a family member underwent a serious surgery. The waiting area was crowded and there were many conversations going on around us. I chatted with this family, asking questions about their family member's condition, and then we gathered together for prayer. After closing the prayer I took my leave but was stopped by a man who sat a few seats away. He politely asked if I had the time to stop and answer a question, and I consented and sat down. This man looked about 40 with hints of silver streaking his thinning hair, trim, fit, and well-dressed. As we engaged in dialogue a sunny intelligence and wry sense of humor colored his words.

He began with a simple, yet polite question: "How does the act of praying with people bring them comfort?" From his sincere tone and serious countenance I knew this was a serious inquiry and not a flip remark aimed to disparage or argue. Smiling, I politely asked if he had ever prayed with or for someone. His reply was negative, with an added rejoinder: "What good would it do?" I continued to politely ask questions and listen to his answers and it became evident he had no spiritual background of any kind. As I patiently listened and answered his questions there was no flicker of emotion, no grasp of spiritual truths. He continued to be polite but distant, engaged but unmoved. When I asked if I might pray for him he kindly refused with a tolerant smile. We shook hands and he thanked me for my time. I left knowing I had sown precious seed to an intelligent hearer, but fearing they had bounced around on the path and were soon devoured by the next book, magazine, or situation that commanded his attention. His heart was hardened by years of exposure to harsh, worldly influences, and he found spiritual topics "banal" and even "childish". Hard ground.

Unreceptive Ground

Path ground is not only unprepared, it's unreceptive. Jesus' words in Matthew 13:19 go beyond mental comprehension to include volitional acceptance. This means the person with a heart of path ground not only doesn't understand what is heard, they do not want to hear or understand (Zechariah 7:12). Matthew 21:33-45 is a great example. In this account the Scribes and Pharisees knew Jesus' parables were about them; they understood His teaching. And yet, they still looked for ways to arrest Him! Their heart was already hardened against anything Jesus had to say. They were prepared beforehand to reject His teaching. His words didn't change them. They couldn't penetrate.

Jesus explained that it is as if such people never heard His words at all. The enemy comes and snatches away any knowledge or memory of God's truth. Maybe you have said these words, or heard others repeat them: "They've been in church all their lives; they've been exposed to bible teaching; how can they live that way now?" The explanation is simple, if tragic. Such people hardened their hearts toward God's truth, refusing to receive it, and it's as if they never heard it. Some even sit through church services refusing to open their hearts to the Word of God. Their mind is made up; they already know they will make no effort to really listen, repent, and surrender.

I've had experiences with such people in the church. Although present for a variety of familial or other reasons, they were completely closed to any spiritual influences. I didn't encounter opposition or problems from such people; they were simply closed to any conversations or influences toward Christ. When pressed or questioned their response was quick, definite, and negative. Such people sat through Sunday School classes, worship services, revival services, and bible studies without allowing anything to penetrate. In most cases, when the familial responsibility was removed, such as with the death of a church-going patriarch, those people never returned to church. Their mind was made up long before. Hard ground.

Plow the Soil

What is the remedy for such hearts? *Plow the soil*. Break up the hardened soil in order to receive good seed. The first step in this process is repentance. When God's Spirit makes one aware of such hardness and indifference, they must make a deliberate turn away from that path and turn toward the path leading to God. God's instructions to Israel through the prophet Hosea are the prescription for path ground.

"*Plant the good seeds of righteousness, and you will harvest a crop of love. Plow up the hard ground of your hearts, for now is the time to seek the Lord, that he may come and shower righteousness upon you."* (Hosea 10:12).

The heart of path ground must return to God's Word with an attitude of openness and surrender to obey. We cannot cause this to happen. When we encounter path ground hearts we must love unconditionally, spread good seed, and trust God's Spirit to plow the dirt. He can and will use our love and service to break up some hard hearts. We cannot discern whom; therefore we must love and serve all.

Protect the Soil

Once the hard heart has been re-broken and cultivated to receive seed, it must be protected from harmful influences that cause hardness. People are accustomed to walking all over it. Stay away from worldly influences. Filter out ungodly input from your ears, eyes, and the mouths of others. Place boundaries around your vulnerable spots: cell phones, computers, reading material, entertainment choices, and relationships. Old associations may need to be severed. Old hangouts may need to be abandoned. Old habits may need to be kicked to the curb and replaced. Don't let anything trample the soil!

"Guard your heart above all else, for it determines the course of your life. Avoid all perverse talk; stay away from corrupt speech. Look straight ahead, and fix your eyes on what lies before you.
Mark out a straight path for your feet; stay on the safe path. Don't get sidetracked; keep your feet from following evil."

(Proverbs 4:23-27)

In the Old Testament, the word "heart" is used more than 800 times. Over 200 times it refers to the thought life, those things that motivate and shape us. The Bible calls this the heart. It's synonymous with our thought life. Why is the thought life so important? King Solomon instructed his son, "Guard your heart above all else" because the thought life controls the rest of your life. Tell me what you think about, and I'll tell you who you are and the life you live. What you think is what you are (Proverbs 23:7).

Your thoughts, whether they be positive, negative, good, or bad, control your attitudes. Your attitudes are the sum total of your thoughts. Attitudes lead to actions. Any good psychologist will tell you that the thought is the father of the deed. Sow a thought, reap a deed. Sow a deed, reap a habit. Sow a habit, reap a character. Sow a character, reap a destiny.

This is so foundational that God destroyed an entire civilization because they had "heart trouble" (Genesis 6:5). God said, "The thoughts of their heart are so evil, I have to destroy them." He sent the flood because of the thoughts of men's hearts. The heart of the human problem is the problem of the human heart. We're still having the same problem they had.

Solomon said to his son, "Guard, protect, and be careful of your thought life." Jesus wants us to present our bodies to Him, including our minds, that He might transform us. No wonder the devil battles for the mind. How important that we learn to keep our hearts, because a fierce battle is raging for the control of your mind. Be careful what enters your mind. Think pure thoughts. Load up on God's Word. Get His truth into your mind and heart (Psalm 119:11).

Chapter 2 – Stony Ground
Matthew 13:5-6, 20-21

Everyone in church circles has witnessed this peculiar phenomenon. Someone comes into the church and soon publicly professes a saving faith in the person and work of Jesus Christ. Immediately they are singing in the choir, working in the nursery, volunteering for this and that, and never missing a service. Onlookers are thrilled at such a fervent and genuine convert. Several months pass and the person encounters adversity. It may or may not be directly connected to their newfound faith. Often it's just life hitting them square in the face, as it does to everyone.

Suddenly, this passionate church-goer, this outspoken advocate for Jesus, is scarce. Their seat is empty; their role in service goes unfulfilled; their offerings remain un-given. And due to the spiritual temperature in most churches, they remain unsought and victims of hindsight. "I knew they wouldn't last." "Well, it must not have been genuine." You've heard it. You've said it. But does anyone wonder why?

When Jesus spoke of rocky soil He wasn't referring to dirt filled with loose stones. Farmers plow up stones and remove them from fields. Every farmer can tell you of the phenomenon of fields growing stones. Jesus was referring to a field consisting of a thin layer of soil with bedrock underneath. When seeds fell upon those kinds of places, it burrowed down into the ground until it hit rock. The roots could go no further, so the plant immediately sprang up because it had no depth of soil.

When a seed goes down into the soil, it decomposes, releases its life in the warmth and moisture of the soil, and begins to germinate. It sends roots down, and a stump or branches up. If the roots hit bedrock and can't go downward, the force of energy moves upward and the plant springs up quicker than normal. A farmer may assume this is the greatest crop yet. However, the roots desperately need water but can't penetrate the rock to get it. The plants looked healthy at first, but when the sun burned hot, they withered because they had no deep root to provide all that was needed. The moisture that was originally in the plant evaporated in the heat of the sun and when the roots tried to get more, there wasn't any way to go down and get it. The plant burned and died and was unproductive.

According to Jesus' explanation, these are people who showed an interest in Jesus and the Word of God. Perhaps they had even benefitted from Him somewhere along the way. They may have been fed, healed, or otherwise served by Him. And in response to His kindness, they make a shallow, emotional response without genuine acceptance. Many are helped by the church and show an initial interest in spiritual things. But when pressure or persecution comes, or difficulties arise related to living a Kingdom lifestyle, they stumble and wither away.

Compare Jesus' farming analogy to something modern. A trip to the chiropractor can make you feel good temporarily; but if the back muscles are not strengthened and toned to keep your back straight, it will go back into a painful misalignment. Occasional trips to the chiropractor make you feel good temporarily, but the root problem is not solved. Occasional trips to church may make you feel good, but the overall problem is not being addressed: there is no rooted faith in, and commitment to, Christ.

It is important to understand the real reason for the death of the plant. It isn't the trial of a scorching sun, but the shallow roots that cannot cope with the trial. The same trial that destroys a shallow plant will prove the quality of another, deeply grounded plant. The sun is absolutely necessary for a plant to grow. Without sunlight the process of photosynthesis cannot take place and the plant will die. So, what proves to be a devastating trial to the plant with shallow roots also proves to be a life-giving source to the plant with deep roots. Therefore, we need to put down roots in order to persevere through life's difficulties.

A ten-year-old boy decided to study judo after losing his left arm in a devastating car accident. The boy began lessons with an old Japanese judo master. He did well, so he couldn't understand why, after three months of training, the master had only taught him one move.

"Sensei," the boy finally said, "Shouldn't I learn more moves?"

"This is the only move you know, but this is the only move you'll ever need to know," the sensei replied. Not quite understanding, but believing in his teacher, the boy kept training.

Several months later, the sensei took the boy to his first tournament. Surprising himself, the boy easily won his first two matches. The third match proved to be more difficult, but after some time, his opponent became impatient and charged; the boy deftly used his one move to win the match.

Still amazed by his success, the boy entered the finals. This time, his opponent was larger, stronger, and much more experienced. For a while, the boy appeared overmatched. Concerned that the boy might get hurt, the referee was about to stop the match when the sensei intervened.

"No," the sensei insisted, "Let him continue."

Soon after the match resumed, his opponent made a critical mistake and dropped his guard. Instantly, the boy used his one move to pin him. The boy had won the match, and the tournament. He was the champion.

As they returned home, the boy and the sensei reviewed every move in each and every match. Then the boy summoned the courage to ask what was really on his mind: "Sensei, how did I win the tournament with only one move?"

"You won for two reasons," the sensei answered. "First, you've almost mastered one of the most difficult throws in all of judo. And second, the only known defense for that move is for your opponent to grab your left arm."

The boy's glaring weakness had become his biggest strength. His roots went down deep as he mastered that one technique. Many Christians wilt when they face the scorching heat of trials because they have shallow roots. They have failed to go on to maturity (Hebrews 6:1). Scripture affirms that we must hold onto the deep truths of the faith (1 Timothy 3:9). A shallow Christianity simply cannot survive times of trouble. A faith that cannot be tested cannot be trusted.

How can we put down roots? Here's a few suggestions:

- <u>Take every opportunity for corporate worship</u> – GO TO CHURCH! We need others' love, encouragement, and support. We need to hear God's Word proclaimed and explained regularly.

- <u>Participate in a small group</u>. We need to follow in the footsteps of mature believers as they follow Christ. We need to experience biblical community. We need to share life with other believers.

- <u>Read the Bible and pray every day</u>. This is as necessary as breathing. Inhale God's truth and exhale your pleas and responses to Him. Every divorce in history began with a communication problem. When communication is cut off there is no meaningful relationship.

- <u>Surrender to complete obedience</u> (James 2:17). If we don't obey what we already know, why should God teach us anything else? Just obey what you know.

Chapter 3 - Thorny Ground
Mathew 13:7, 22

Weeds. My father had a passion for weeds. He didn't love them; he hated them. But he loved having a young son at home to remove weeds from our summer vegetable garden. Every. Single. Weed. Sometimes I had trouble telling weeds from vegetable plants, like corn. Do you realize that young corn plants and Johnson grass look exactly the same?

Verse 7 is the shortest line in the entire account, and yet the weeds it describe perpetrate the most damage. The 'thorns' here are various types of weeds that spring up and choke the good seed plants. Because weeds grow higher and faster than good plants, they block out and absorb more sunlight while consuming water and nutrients the good plants need. Every gardener knows the unending battle to keep weeds from taking over and destroying everything good.

In Jesus' story these weeds are the worries of life and the lure of wealth (vs. 22) that crowd out any time or attention given to spiritual growth or Kingdom concerns. Instead of being driven from the truth by hardship (as in the stony ground), this person is drawn away from the truth by the promise of something better. Just like the Johnson grass in our family garden, these weeds appear to be something good. Most of us want to be respectable, well-to-do citizens who take good care of our families and are able to set aside money for the kids' college and nice vacations. What's wrong with that? Because these things resemble blessings from God, we pursue them and ask God to bring them to pass as

His blessing. But in our pursuit of them we neglect eternally-valuable matters such as discipleship, spiritual growth, holiness, and evangelism.

The Worries of Life

Life is filled with detours, dead-ends, and difficulties. Jesus warned us about becoming consumed with such things in Matthew 6:25-34. Read through it slowly below:

"That is why I tell you not to worry about everyday life—whether you have enough food and drink, or enough clothes to wear. Isn't life more than food, and your body more than clothing? Look at the birds. They don't plant or harvest or store food in barns, for your heavenly Father feeds them. And aren't you far more valuable to him than they are? Can all your worries add a single moment to your life? And why worry about your clothing? Look at the lilies of the field and how they grow. They don't work or make their clothing, yet Solomon in all his glory was not dressed as beautifully as they are. And if God cares so wonderfully for wildflowers that are here today and thrown into the fire tomorrow, he will certainly care for you. Why do you have so little faith? So don't worry about these things, saying, 'What will we eat? What will we drink? What will we wear?' These things dominate the thoughts of unbelievers, but your heavenly Father already knows all your needs. Seek the Kingdom of God above all else, and live righteously, and he will give you everything you need. So don't worry about tomorrow, for tomorrow will bring its own worries. Today's trouble is enough for today."

Included in these cares of the world are worldly pursuits, all the activities involving our kids, and anything that competes with a Kingdom focus. Allowing ourselves to become consumed with the cares of this world opens the door for the second weed Jesus listed.

The Lure of Wealth

Money is deceitful because it makes promises it cannot keep.

- "If I had more money I would have no problems."
- "If I had more money it would take care of my other problems."
- "If I could just get ahead and breathe a little, I could focus on serving the Lord."
- "Once I get my debts paid off, then I can support the Lord's work."
- "It costs money to provide _____ for my family."
- "I want to give my kids all the things I never had."

When we are consumed with the cares of this life we easily believe these lies and chase after wealth, entertainment, and popularity; more commonly known as 'the American Dream'. So easily we fall into this trap! We see what others have and focus on what we don't have. The neighbor up the street drives a beautiful new truck with plenty of room inside for his family and plenty of hauling space for his vast collection of hunting and fishing equipment. He waves as he passes my home daily on his way to the lake or the woods. My daydream of his existence is filled with catching fish, taking game, and enjoying life to the fullest, all while driving around in that beautiful truck (do you see how it keeps showing up?). I see only a snapshot of his life and my imagination fills in the rest with all the things I desire. How do I know he's really happy? What if he escapes to the woods or lake daily to avoid a terrible family situation? What if the truck I envy (there it is again!) was purchased with an insurance settlement from the death of a child?

Do you see how this game works? You may not be enticed by vehicles or outdoor sports equipment, but there is always something appealing that can cross your vision and press the "I want that" button within. Before long, we're telling ourselves how wretched our lives are and how vastly improved they would be if we only had _____. By then we've fallen into the pit of depending on things to bring us satisfaction. That never works. If it did, most stores would be out of business and there would be few, if any, yard sales.

Examine these Scriptures carefully:

- *"Then he said, Beware! Guard against every kind of greed. Life is not measured by how much you own."* Luke 12:15

- *"For the love of money is the root of all kinds of evil. And some people, craving money, have wandered from the true faith and pierced themselves with many sorrows."* 1 Timothy 6:10

- *"No one can serve two masters. For you will hate one and love the other; you will be devoted to one and despise the other. You cannot serve both God and money."* Matthew 6:24

- *"Don't wear yourself out trying to get rich. Be wise enough to know when to quit. In the blink of an eye wealth disappears, for it will sprout wings and fly away like an eagle."* Proverbs 23:4-5

- *"Do not love this world nor the things it offers you, for when you love the world, you do not have the love of the Father in you. For the world offers only a craving for physical pleasure, a craving for everything we see, and pride in our achievements and possessions. These are not from the Father, but are from this world. And this world is fading away, along with everything that people crave. But anyone who does what pleases God will live forever."* 1 John 2:15-17

Do you get it? We're not wired to obtain satisfaction from inanimate objects or even from human relationships. While these things can bring us some pleasure, they also come with their own set of heartaches and disappointments. People will let you down. They make hurtful mistakes. Toys wear out or break, or there's a new upgrade that makes yours outmoded and dull. You know this is true, don't you? How long did it take for the new to wear off that shiny new truck (there it is again!)? When the first payment was due? When someone crashed into it? That empty feeling that followed soon after the newness wore off is the internal signal that nothing can ultimately satisfy us except a vibrant relationship with Jesus Christ.

Pulling the Weeds

How do we pull these insidious weeds that compete with our loyalty to Christ? Look in your datebook and your checkbook. Where does your time and money go? If you cannot attend church faithfully, serve the Lord faithfully, give to God's work faithfully, maintain personal discipleship and disciple others faithfully, then you are being faithful to someone or something else. That someone or something else is a weed. Pull it out!

How do I know if something is a weed? Corn and Johnson grass look the same, at first. So do legitimate pursuits and life-stealing weeds. Do I desire a new truck because I believe it will bring me pleasure or because I need a vehicle to transport my family and me to necessary destinations? Is a vehicle really meant to do anything else? Why do I want a larger house? Is it for satisfying my ego or for utilitarian reasons? Do I really need 6 fishing poles, 4 rifles, 2 boats, and all the accessories that are available for each?

Ask the Holy Spirit to reveal whose agenda you are pursuing. Consuming worry is not from God; nor is the relentless pursuit of 'getting ahead'.

Trust Jesus with every facet of your life. Faith creates fertile soil where the truth of God can grow and bear fruit. Remember Jesus' admonition in the passage we read above? *"Seek the Kingdom of God above all else, and live righteously, and he will give you everything you need."*

- Lord, I trust you with my needs (not my greeds).
- Lord, I trust you with my family.
- Lord I trust you with my eternity.
- Lord, I trust you with my tomorrow.

Here's one more:

- Lord, I trust you about the truck.....

Chapter 4 - Good Ground
Matthew 13:8, 23

Jesus made it clear that every person's spiritual heart condition is represented by one of these four types of soil. Path ground pictures hardened hearts that refuse to understand God's Word. Their minds are already made up and they are unwilling to listen or change. Stony ground pictures hearts that have shown an emotional, shallow response to the gospel. When trouble comes they stumble and wither away and bear no fruit. Thorny (weedy) ground pictures hearts that allow the concerns of this life and the pursuit of wealth to choke out the Word before it can grow and produce fruit.

We finally reach the good ground in Matthew 7:8, 23. This person's heart is open to receiving the seed of God's Word and displays a willingness to obey. Hearing is never enough; there must be an intent toward obedience as well (James 1:22).

Due to their openness, this person puts down roots, gaining depth of understanding and resulting obedience. They actively pull weeds, removing anything that competes with loyalty to Christ. They bear fruits of holiness and righteousness from precious seed (see Matthew 7:20; John 15:5, 8).

This is who we want to be, right? This type of heart is what we desire and what Christ desires for us. If only there weren't so many obstacles in the way!

Here are two suggestions to maintain good fertile soil for receiving God's Word:

Avoid the problems in the parable. Avoid a willful lack of understanding and acceptance. Avoid emotional responses without genuine acceptance. Avoid worried preoccupation with the world and wealth. Choose faith instead. Choose to listen and trust in God's Word and allow it to have its perfect work within you. Choose to learn, deliberately obey, and embrace God's plan for your life. Choose to be thankful for what God provides and to hold everything loosely.

I must take another opportunity here to emphasize the importance of membership and active participation in a local church. My pastor is fond of repeating, "God is still writing your story." In fact, those attending worship each week face those words as they enter the worship center.

God is *still* writing your story...
NORTHRIDGENETWORK.COM

Regular engagement with a small group doing life together provides encouragement and accountability that is needed as we seek to grow as a disciple and avoid the problems outlined by Jesus in this parable. Who are you meeting with regularly to study, pray, laugh, struggle, eat, play, grow, cry, challenge, serve, and worship? If you are habitually engaged with other growing believers in all the above activities, you will have better success maintaining fertile ground for spiritual growth and vitality.

<u>Anticipate varied levels of fruit-bearing</u>. Jesus chose fruit-bearing as an illustration of Christian growth and service for a reason. Fruit-bearing is seasonal. Fruit grows in different seasons and so our fruitfulness will vary in different seasons of our lives (Ecclesiastes 3:1-2).

Would you expect a tiny, young sapling, still green and with no bark, to produce fruit? In early stages it's more likely that others will have to care for the plant and water it, shelter it, and be sure it gets enough sunlight.

Even when a tree is still young, it may be getting stronger, developing protective bark, and increasing in height, but it's still quite small and immature. It's not as incredibly delicate as the sapling, but it's certainly not ready to bear the hundred-fold increase God has promised.

After long and difficult preparation, God will eventually bring His children into a season of fruitfulness. After we demonstrate faithfulness, and pass through much testing, after building up our faith, God can use us.

Fruit-bearing is progressive. Just as cultivation, irrigation, and fertilization can improve a crop over seasons, so we can strive to become more fruitful over time. As we walk by faith, practice the spiritual disciplines, and live lives of obedience, we should see increasing levels of fruitfulness. Only the tests of time, perseverance, and the presence of fruit can prove a profession is genuine.

These seasons of fruitfulness don't have to come only after many years of preparation. The analogy only stretches so far. We are not trees. We're people whom God loves and for whom Jesus died, and within whom His Holy Spirit miraculously works every moment. As God works and we learn and obey, He will produce fruit. Small harvests at first, and increasing harvests as we mature.

> *"Still other seeds fell on fertile soil, and they produced a crop that was thirty, sixty, and even a hundred times as much as had been planted!"* Matthew 13:8

Chapter 5 - Dull Hearts
Matthew 13:10-17

Jesus ended His initial telling of the Parable of the Sower with these words (verse 9): "Anyone with ears to hear should listen and understand." When His disciples asked Him about the use of parables to teach the multitudes, Jesus' response stems from his statement in verse 9. In fact, He made that statement many times throughout the gospels. Having 'ears to hear' doesn't refer to possessing physical ears that are fully functional, but rather to one's willingness to listen with a mind to learn and a heart to obey. I call it having "surrendered ears."

As Jesus further explained in our focal passage of Matthew 13, the disciples were granted understanding of the "secrets of the Kingdom of Heaven" (verse 11) due to their willingness to listen to Jesus with a heart inclined toward obedience. This willingness would cause them to have a growing understanding of Kingdom truth (verse 12a).

However, not everyone has "surrendered ears." Many heard Jesus that day but did not understand the truths of His parables because their hearts were "hardened" toward Him (verse 15). It is clearly implied by the wording of these verses that such hardness stemmed from deliberate action. They willfully ceased from hearing and seeking God's truth, in order that their lives not be changed.

Why wouldn't anyone want to understand God's truth and be changed? Their hearts are already hard, and their mind is made up (path ground). Their profession of faith was emotional and shallow, not lasting or genuine (stony ground). They have allowed other things to crowd out their loyalty to Christ (thorny ground).

This begs an important question: are these 'hard-hearted' people believers or non-believers? With path ground it's obvious. The ground is hard, there is no plant, no fruit, and a complete rejection of the seed. To me, the stony ground is equally obvious. It's shallow, allowing no root and therefore no plant or fruit.

But what about the thorny (weedy) ground? According to Jesus' analogy, there was some initial growth, and even some fruit-bearing, before the weeds of life crowded out any long-term growth. The Holman Christian Standard Bible captures the translation well in verse 22 where Jesus says the plant in thorny (weedy) ground "becomes unfruitful", therefore implying an early stage of fruitfulness that was never carried out to maturity. Such a person could be a genuine believer and yet allow the cares of this life or the pursuit of wealth to choke out any genuine fruitfulness.

"Anyone who builds on that foundation may use a variety of materials—gold, silver, jewels, wood, hay, or straw. But on the judgment day, fire will reveal what kind of work each builder has done. The fire will show if a person's work has any value. If the work survives, that builder will receive a reward. But if the work is burned up, the builder will suffer great loss. The builder will be saved, but like someone barely escaping through a wall of flames." 1 Corinthians 3:12-15

Taking these truths literally, thorny (weedy) ground people could be genuine believers that have never moved on past infancy. Or, they could be genuine believers who, after a period of fruit-bearing, became enmeshed with weeds that choked out any spiritual focus. In Jesus' interpretation of the parable there are four types of soil but only two categories of response: true faith or core unbelief that is revealed immediately or over time.

Has your heart grown dull? Is there lasting fruit (evidence) of the Holy Spirit's work in your life? Do you have full faith and assurance that you are a child of God by repentance and faith? Do you need to seek assurance of your relationship with Christ? Do you need to recommit yourself to fully following Jesus?

Summary

When speaking in a public forum on religious topics, whether in a church or some other venue, I notice the same pattern. I can tell how well (or not) I'm communicating the message by how the audience reacts. People who will not make eye contact, who whisper to those around them, who thumb through other material, who sit the whole time with crossed arms and stony looks, or who frequently check their watches or phones—these people aren't getting the message. I might as well be sowing seed outside on the asphalt or concrete parking lot.

With other people, I've been thrilled as their eyes lit up with delight because they comprehended the message. When I was through, they shook my hand vigorously and praised me for the insightful message and bubbled on about how it would change their life. Then a few days later, I encountered them at a different location, and they didn't recognize me or recall anything I said. When I attempted to help them recapture the excitement they had after hearing my message, they waved it off in boredom. They are like the seed that falls on shallow ground.

Then there have been those whose eyes light up just as brightly as I spoke, but there was a sad undertone about their expression. They greeted me after with praise for the message, but I could sense that something troubled them inside. Later I discovered they were so overwhelmed with problems that they felt as if they were drowning. Like seed among thorns, I believe they wanted to accept the message, but they didn't want to let go of the problems in their lives that stood in the way.

But there were people who accepted the message with intelligent eyes, greeted me afterward with a word of thanks, and shot out the door to put what they heard into practice. Years later, I've bumped into them or received a message via email or social media, and they recalled the message, recounted what it meant to them, and thanked me again. This has happened to me. A man I didn't remember walked up to me at a social function and thanked me for a sermon I had preached in his church a year or two before. He could remember it well enough to explain to me how he had put it into practice and what a difference it made to him and others. Another time a man told me that he had attended a conference I led about a year before, had returned to his church and implemented what he had learned, and wanted to share the results with me. He was thrilled over how it was working. These are seeds that fell on fertile ground.

Which of these people are you? More importantly, which one do you wish to be? If you aspire to be anything but good ground I'm surprised you reached the end of this book. If you're still here, there must be a desire deep down to become fertile soil bearing much fruit for Christ's Kingdom. So, what's stopping you?

About the Author

Michael Stover is a husband to one, father of five, and new grandfather. Since 2006 he has written, edited, and contributed to numerous Bible study materials, websites, college subject matter, blogs, fiction, poetry, and nonfiction works. Michael holds degrees from Union University and Mid-America Baptist Theological Seminary, both in his home state of Tennessee. In addition to freelance writing and editing, Michael enjoys reading, fishing, cooking, and lots of family time.

Visit Michael's website at www.michaeldstover.com.

Follow Michael on Twitter at @michaeldstover

Also by the Author

Have you ever wanted to improve your writing skills? Why is it important to write well? It seems like a silly question, but our writings precede us. When applying for a job we must submit a resume' and sometimes a cover letter. Or how about when sending e-mails to people we don't know well or haven't met, such as work partners, customers, or when responding on behalf of your company or institute? Your writing often forms the first impression, and you only get one chance to make it. When writing, we send a message about ourselves.

Michael has distilled over 10 years of writing and editing experience into one easy-to-read work that you will refer to again and again. Learn from his simple lessons and realize a marked improvement in your writing after just the first 30 minutes!

Get yours today in print or digital form from your favorite bookseller!

For more about how Michael can help you with Copywriting, Copy Editing, or Proofreading, email michaeldstover70@gmail.com or book a FREE consultation online.

Also, Subscribe to Michael's monthly newsletter and get a FREE list of writing tips!

Keep up with the author and new writing projects at www.michaeldstover.com

Appendix - Sermon Outlines for the Parable of the Sower

Pastors, use these sermon outlines to share The Parable of the Sower with your church. They are the skeleton from which this book was formed. Hang your own meat on them and make them your own!

Path Ground - Message 1

Matthew 13:3-4, 18-19

<u>Series Introduction</u>: New Series on Old Truths. Nothing new, but reexamining old truths. We tend to forget.

<u>Opening Illustration</u>: Preacher & little boy, boy cannot start lawnmower, preacher rides up on a bike and offers to trade the bike for the mower. They trade. Next day boy rides by on the bike and the preacher is trying to start the mower. "I think I got a bad deal, this mower won't start." Little boy, "You have to cuss it before it will start." Preacher, "I'm a preacher, I don't cuss; I forgot how to cuss a long time ago." Boy, "Keep cranking that mower preacher, it will come back to ya!"

It is my hope and prayer that as we reexamine these truths together it will "come back to you".

Simple explanation of the analogy

- Seed - Word of God
- Sower - Jesus, Us

- Soils - Hearts of men, having different levels of receptivity

"We've got the dirt on everyone!" Everyone's heart condition is represented by one of these 4 types of soil. That is the focus of this message series.

I. Path Soil (vs. 3-4, 18-19)

   A. <u>Untilled</u> Ground

      1. 'Wayside' was the path between or around fields.

      2. It was hardened by walking, carrying or transporting burdens by pack animals, baked by the sun, etc.

   B. <u>Unprepared</u> for Seed

      1. No prior efforts or preparations had been made to in any way make the soil ready to receive seed.

      2. This heart is hardened by constant exposure to negative elements.

         a. Trodden down by harsh realities of life

         b. Pummeled by course interactions with people

         c. Baked and scorched by the hot, searing effects of willful sin

   Not only unprepared, it is:

   C. <u>Unreceptive</u>

      1. "...does not 'understand' it" (vs. 19)

2. This word goes beyond mere mental comprehension to include volitional acceptance.

3. It means the person with this heart of Path Ground "Doesn't want to hear and accept" the Truth of God.

4. Example: Matthew 21:33-45

    a. Their heart was already hardened to anything Jesus had to say.

    b. They were prepared beforehand to reject it!

    c. It didn't change them.

5. Now the enemy comes and snatches away any knowledge or memory of God's Truth (vs. 4b, 19b)

6. It becomes as if they never heard it at all.

- "They have been in church all their lives, been exposed to the Truth; how can they live that way now?" They hardened their hearts toward the Truth, refusing to receive it, and it is as if they never heard it.

- Some sit through church services today refusing to open their hearts to the Word of God; their mind is made up, they already know they will make no effort to really listen, repent, and surrender.

II. Plow the Soil

A. <u>Repent</u> of hardness and rejecting God's Word - Hosea 10:12

1. Repent means to turn *away* from something and *toward* something else.

2. Breaking with old attitudes and perceptions is the important first step to opening up your heart to God.

3. When we are willing to become open, the Holy Spirit will work with is to soften our hardened heart.

B. <u>Return</u> to God's Word with an attitude of openness and surrender - Exodus 19:8

1. After turning away from our life without God, we now turn toward Him and His Word.

2. God promises to use His Word to accomplish His purposes for us and within us when we accept and obey it. Isaiah 55:11

III. Protect the Soil

People are accustomed to walking all over it. After you have tilled it up to receive the seed, protect it from harmful influences that cause hardness.

1. Stay away from sinful influences

2. Filter out ungodly input (ears, eyes, mouth)

3. Don't let anything bad get into the soil!

Stony Ground - Message 2

Matthew 13:5-6, 20-21

Opening Illustration: There is a story of a farm boy who accidentally overturned his wagonload of corn in the road. The farmer who lived nearby came to investigate. "Hey, Willis," he called out, "forget your troubles for a spell and come on in and have dinner with us. Then I'll help you get the wagon up." "That's mighty nice of you," Willis answered, "But I don't think Pa would like me to." "Aw, come on, son!" the farmer insisted. "Well, okay," the boy finally agreed. "But Pa won't like it." After a hearty dinner, Willis thanked his host. "I feel a lot better now, but I just know Pa is going to be real upset." "Don't be foolish!" exclaimed the neighbor. "By the way, where is he?" "Under the wagon."

I don't want to run off and leave anyone "under the wagon" while we move on, so permit me a moment to review last week:

Matthew 13:1-9, 18-23 - Simple explanation of the analogy

- Seed - Word of God

- Sower - Jesus, Us

- Soils - Hearts of men, having different levels of receptivity

"We've got the dirt on everyone!" Everyone's heart condition is represented by one of these 4 types of soil. That is the focus of this message series.

Week 1: Path Ground = hardened hearts that refuse to understand God's Word; minds are already made up; not willing to listen or change.

Week 2: <u>Stony Ground</u>

I. Stony Ground

   A. Explanation

      1. "Not much earth" (vs. 5) meaning a thin layer of soil with bedrock underneath

      2. Therefore the plants looked healthy at the first, but when the sun burned hot, they withered because they "had no root" (vs. 6)

   B. Application

      1. These are people who showed an interest in Jesus and the Word; perhaps they had benefitted from Him (healing, feeding, etc.)

      2. They make a shallow, emotional response without genuine acceptance (roots).

      3. Many are helped by the church and show an initial interest in spiritual things.

      4. When pressure or persecution comes, or difficulties related to living the Kingdom lifestyle, they "stumble" (vs. 21) and "wither away" (vs. 6).

      5. <u>Illustration</u>: Trip to the Chiropractor can make you feel good temporarily; but if the back muscles are not

strengthened and toned to keep your back straight, it will go back into a painful misalignment. Occasional trips to the chiropractor make you feel good temporarily, but the root problem is not solved. Occasional trips to church may make you feel good, but the overall problem is not being addressed: there is no rooted faith in and commitment to Christ.

II. Roots are Essential

A. It is important to understand that the real reason the plant dies is not because of the trial of the scorching sun, but because it doesn't have deep enough roots to deal with the trial.

1. The same trial that destroys one plant will prove the quality of another plant. Everything depends on the roots.

2. If the roots are shallow the plant will be scorched and die. However, if the roots are deep, the plant will survive and its very survival proves that it is a strong, healthy plant.

3. The sun is absolutely necessary for a plant to grow. Without the sunlight the process of photosynthesis cannot take place and the plant will die.

4. So what proves to be a devastating trial to the plant with shallow roots also proves to be a life giving source to the plant with deep roots. We need to put

down roots so that we can persevere in the face of difficulties.

   B. Judo Illustration from Chapter 2

      1. The reason that so many Christians wilt when they face the scorching heat of trials and tribulations is that they have shallow root systems.

      2. They have failed to "go on to maturity" (Hebrews 6:1).

      3. The Bible teaches us that it is very important that we "keep hold of the deep truths of the faith" (1 Timothy 3:9). A shallow Christianity simply cannot survive times of trouble.

III. How to Put Down Roots

   A. Take Every Opportunity for Corporate Worship/Bible Study/Fellowship - GO TO CHURCH!!

      1. We need others' love, encouragement, and support.

      2. We need to follow in the footsteps of other mature believers as they follow Christ.

      3. We need to hear the Word of God proclaimed and explained regularly.

   B. Read the bible & Pray Every Day

      1. This is as necessary as breathing! It is life!

      2. Inhale God's Truth and exhale your pleas and responses to Him.

3. There has never been a divorce in history where there wasn't a problem with communication. When communication is cut off there can be no meaningful relationship.

C. Surrender to Complete Obedience

1. James 2:17

2. If we don't obey what we know, why should God teach us anything else?

Is your heart like Stony Ground? Shallow, emotional, but uncommitted? No deep roots of faith? *Put down roots!*

Thorny Ground - Message 3

Matthew 13:7,22

Opening Illustration: A very zealous soul-winning young preacher recently came upon a farmer working in his field. Being concerned about the farmer's soul the preacher asked the man, "Are you laboring in the vineyard of the Lord my good man?" Not even looking at the preacher and continuing his work the farmer replied, "Naw, these are soybeans." "You don't understand," said the preacher. "Are you a Christian?" With the same amount of interest as his previous answer the farmer said, "Nope my name is Jones. You must be lookin' for Jim Christian. He lives a mile south of here." The young determined preacher tried again asking the farmer, "Are you lost?" "Naw! I've lived here all my life," answered the farmer. "Are you prepared for the resurrection?" the frustrated preacher asked. This caught the farmer's attention and he asked, "When's it gonna be?" Thinking he had accomplished something the young preacher replied, "It could be today, tomorrow, or the next day." Taking a handkerchief from his back pocket and wiping his brow, the farmer remarked, "Well, don't mention it to my wife. She don't get out much and she'll wanna go all three days."

I want to thank and congratulate those of you who are here for week three of this series; you've been here all three days!

Matthew 13:1-9, 18-23 - Simple explanation of the analogy

- Seed - Word of God
- Sower - Jesus, Us

- Soils - Hearts of men, having different levels of receptivity

Everyone's heart condition is represented by one of these 4 types of soil. That is the focus of this message series.

Week 1: Path Ground = hardened hearts that refuse to understand God's Word; minds are already made up; not willing to listen or change.

Week 2: Stony Ground = hearts that have shown an emotional, shallow response to the Gospel, but when trouble comes, they stumble and wither away, bearing no fruit.

Week 3: **Thorny Ground**

    I.   Thorny Ground

        A. Explanation

            1. 'Thorns' (vs. 7) are weeds that spring up and 'choke' the good seed plants.

            2. The weeds consume the water and nutrients that the plants need.

            3. Weeds grow higher and faster than good plants, blocking and absorbing more sunlight.

        B. Application

            1. 'Cares of this world' and 'the deceitfulness of riches' (vs. 22) crowd out any time or attention given to spiritual growth or Kingdom concerns.

2. Instead of being driven from the truth by hardship (as in the Stony Ground), this person is lured away from the truth by the promise of something better.

II. Weeds Mean Death

    A. The Cares of This World

        1. Life always has complications and difficulties.

        2. Matthew 6:25-33

        3. Included in these cares of the world are worldly pursuits, all the different things our kids can be involved in now, anything that competes with a Kingdom focus.

        4. Allowing ourselves to become consumed with the 'cares of this world' opens the door for the second weed listed:

    B. The Deceitfulness of Riches

        1. Riches are deceitful because they make promises they cannot keep.

            a. If I had more money I would have no problems.

            b. If I had more money it would take care of my other problems.

            c. If I could just get ahead and breathe a little, I could focus on serving the Lord.

            d. Once I get my debts paid off, then I can support the Lord's work.

e. It costs money to provide _____ for my kids/family.

f. I want to give them all the things I never had......

2. When we are consumed with the 'cares of this world' we easily believe these lies and chase after wealth, entertainment, popularity, and prosperity; more commonly known as "The American Dream".

III. Pulling the Weeds

A. Remove Anything that Competes with Your Loyalty to Christ

1. Look in your datebook

2. Look in your checkbook

3. If you cannot attend church faithfully, serve the Lord faithfully, give to God's work faithfully, then you are being faithful to someone or something else.

4. That something else is a weed. Pull it out!

B. Trust Him With Every Part of Your Life

1. Faith creates fertile soil where the Truth of God can grow and bear fruit.

a. Lord, I trust you with my needs (not my greeds).

b. Lord, I trust you with my family.

c. Lord, I trust you with my eternity.

  d. Lord. I trust you with my tomorrow.

2. Matthew 6:33

Good Ground - Message 4

Matthew 13:8-9,23

Opening Illustrations (2): A busload of politicians were driving down a country road, when suddenly the bus ran off the road and crashed into an old farmer's barn. The old farmer got off his tractor and went to investigate. Soon he dug a hole and buried the politicians. A few days later, the local sheriff came out, saw the crashed bus and asked the old farmer where all the politicians had gone. The old farmer told him he had buried them. The sheriff asked the old farmer, "Lordy, were they ALL dead?" The old farmer said, "Well, some of them said they weren't, but you know how them crooked politicians lie."

Two rednecks meet on a dusty country road. One of them is carrying a big bag labeled, "chickens." "Chickens, eh?" says one guy. "Hey, if I guess how many chickens you got, will you give me one?" "Shooooot," says the guy with the bag, "iffin you guess right, I'll give you both of 'em."

I'm glad we don't have to rely on the twisted opinions of people, or our own guesses, to know how to be fruitful believers! In Jesus' Parable of the Sower in Matthew 13 He teaches us about how the hearts of people can differ regarding how they are open to God's Word.

Matthew 13:1-9, 18-23 - Simple explanation of the analogy

- Seed - Word of God
- Sower - Jesus, Us

- Soils - Hearts of men, having different levels of receptivity

Everyone's heart condition is represented by one of these 4 types of soil. That is the focus of this message series.

Week 1: Path Ground = hardened hearts that refuse to understand God's Word; minds are already made up; not willing to listen or change.

Week 2: Stony Ground = hearts that have shown an emotional, shallow response to the Gospel, but when trouble comes, they stumble and wither away, bearing no fruit.

Week 3: Thorny Ground = hearts that allow the concerns of this life and the pursuit of wealth to choke out the Word before it can grow and produce fruit.

Week 4: **Good Ground**

    I. **Aspire to Good Ground**

        A. Hears

            1. Plow the Soil

            2. Openness to the Word & Willingness to Obey

        B. Understands

            1. Puts Down Roots, Gaining depth of Understanding & Obedience

            2. Pulls Weeds, removing anything that competes with loyalty to Christ

        C. Bears Fruit

1. Matthew 7:20
2. John 15:5
3. John 15:8

II. Avoid the Problems in the Parable

A. Willful Lack of Understanding & Acceptance (Path Ground)

B. Emotional Response Without Genuine Acceptance (Stony Ground)

C. Worry & Preoccupation with the Word & Wealth (Thorny Ground)

Use points from previous outlines to emphasize each

III. Anticipate Varied Levels of Fruit-Bearing

Jesus chose fruit-bearing as an illustration of Christian growth & service for a reason.

It is:

A. Seasonal

1. Just as fruit grows in different seasons, so our fruitfulness can and will vary in different seasons of our lives.
2. Ecclesiastes 3:1-2

   a. Infancy

      i. Would you expect a tiny young sapling, still green and with no bark at all, to produce fruit? In this early stage, it is more than likely that others would have to care for the tree, and water it, shelter it, and make sure that it gets enough sunlight and has no weeds to choke its feeble roots.

    ii. 1 Peter 2:2

b. Intermediate Growth

    i. Even as a tree is still young, it may be getting stronger, and develop protective bark, and increase in height, but it's still quite small and immature. It's not as incredibly delicate as the sapling in the previous season, but it's certainly not ready to bear the hundred-fold increase of fruit that God has promised.

    ii. Hebrews 5:13-14

c. Maturity

    i. After a long (and many times difficult) preparation, God will eventually bring His children into a season of fruitfulness. After demonstrating much faithfulness, and passing through much testing, and after the building up of our faith, God can use us.

    ii. Psalm 1:1-3

B. Progressive

1. Just as cultivation, irrigation, and fertilization can improve a crop over seasons, so can we strive to be more fruitful over time.

2. As we walk by faith, practice the spiritual disciplines, and live lives of obedience, we should see increasing levels of fruitfulness.

Only the tests of time, perseverance, and the presence of fruit can prove a profession is genuine.

Dull Hearts - Message 5

Matthew 13:10-17

In Jesus' Parable of the Sower in Matthew 13 He teaches how the hearts of people differ regarding how open they are to God's Word.

- Seed - Word of God
- Sower - Jesus, Us
- Soils - Hearts of men, having different levels of receptivity

Everyone's heart condition is represented by one of these 4 types of soil. That is the focus of this message series.

Week 1: Path Ground = hardened hearts that refuse to understand God's Word; minds are already made up; not willing to listen or change.

Week 2: Stony Ground = hearts that have shown an emotional, shallow response to the Gospel, but when trouble comes, they stumble and wither away, bearing no fruit.

Week 3: Thorny Ground = hearts that allow the concerns of this life and the pursuit of wealth to choke out the Word before it can grow and produce fruit.

Week 4: Good Ground = hearts that are ready and receptive to God's Truth, with a full intent to surrender and obey.

    I.   **Surrendered Ears**

A. Jesus ended His initial telling of the Parable of the Sower with these words (verse 9): "*He who has ears to hear, let him hear!*" When His disciples asked Him about His use of parables to teach the multitudes, Jesus' response stems from His statement in verse 9.

    1. Jesus makes this statement many times throughout the Gospels.

    2. "Having ears to hear" does not refer to one's possession of physical hearing capabilities, but rather to one's willingness to listen with a mind to learn and a heart to obey. It is having "surrendered ears".

B. The disciples were granted understanding of the 'mysteries of the kingdom'

    1. Because of their willingness to listen to Jesus, with a heart willing to learn and obey.

    2. And this willingness would cause them to have a growing understanding of kingdom truth (vs. 12a).

However, not everyone has "surrendered ears".

II. Dull hearts

A. They would not understand the kingdom truths behind Jesus' parables because their hearts "have grown dull" (vs. 15).

    1. It is clearly implied by the wording of these verses that such dullness has stemmed from

deliberate action on the part of the potential hearers.

2. They have deliberately ceased from hearing and seeing God's truth, so that their lives will not be changed by it (vs. 15).

B. Why wouldn't anyone want to understand God's truth and be changed by it? Why would we deliberately have 'Dull Hearts'?

1. Our hearts are already hard; our minds made up (Path Ground)

2. Our profession of faith was emotional and shallow, not lasting or genuine (Stony Ground)

3. We have allowed other things to crowd out our loyalty to Christ (Thorny Ground)

C. Are these 'Dull-Hearted' people believers or non-believers?

1. Path Ground - hard, no plant, no fruit, complete rejection

2. Stony Ground - shallow, emotional response, no fruit, no lasting result

3. Thorny Ground - some initial growth, but the weeds of life crowd out any real growth

   a. 'Becomes' unfruitful (vs. 22) implying a start at fruitfulness that was never carried out to maturity.

b. 1 Corinthians 3:12-15

c. Thorny Ground could be genuine believers that have never moved on past infancy, or could be lost.

4. In Jesus' interpretation of the parable there are four soils but only two basic categories of response:

a. True Faith

b. Core Unbelief - revealed immediately or over time

Has your heart 'grown dull'?

- Is there lasting fruit/evidence of the Spirit's work in your life?

- Do you have full faith and assurance that you are a child of God?

- Do you need to seek assurance of your salvation?

- Do you need to recommit yourself to fully following Jesus?

Bonus Message - (Use this outline as a stand-alone message or to rehash the series)

Cultivating Your Soil

How to Cultivate Your Heart for a Spiritual Harvest

Matthew 13

I. **Plow the Soil - Repentance & Recommitment / Salvation**

   A. Path Ground - Hard Hearts

      1. Trodden down by harsh realities of life

      2. Pummeled by course interactions with people

      3. Baked and scorched by the hot, searing effects of willful sin

      4. Not only unprepared, it is Unreceptive. Doesn't want to hear or accept.

   B. Breaking Up Ground

      1. <u>Repent</u> of hardness and rejecting God's Word

      2. Hosea 10:12

      3. <u>Return</u> to God's Word with an attitude of openness and surrender

II. **Put Down Roots - Seek Depth in Your Walk with Christ**

   A. Stony Ground - No Roots

1. These are people who showed an interest in Jesus and the Word; perhaps they had benefitted from Him (healing, feeding, etc.)

2. They make a shallow, emotional response without genuine acceptance (roots).

3. Many are helped by the church and show an initial interest in spiritual things.

4. When pressure or persecution comes, or difficulties related to living the Kingdom lifestyle, they "stumble" (vs. 21) and "wither away" (vs. 6).

B. Putting Down Roots

1. Take Every Opportunity for Corporate Worship/Bible Study/Fellowship - GO TO CHURCH!!

2. Read the bible & Pray Every Day

3. Surrender to Complete Obedience

4. James 2:17

III. Pull the Weeds - Remove Hindrances/Temptations/Obstacles to Spiritual Growth

A. Thorny Ground

1. Life always has complications and difficulties

2. Included in these cares of the world are worldly pursuits, all the different things our kids can be

involved in now, anything that competes with a Kingdom focus.

3. Allowing ourselves to become consumed with the 'cares of this world' opens the door for the second weed listed: the Deceitfulness of Riches

4. Riches are deceitful because they make promises they cannot keep.

5. When we are consumed with the 'cares of this world' we easily believe these lies and chase after wealth, entertainment, popularity, and prosperity; more commonly known as "The American Dream".

B. Pulling the Weeds

1. Remove Anything that Competes with Your Loyalty to Christ

   a. Look in your datebook

   b. Look in your checkbook

   c. If you cannot attend church faithfully, serve the Lord faithfully, give to God's work faithfully, then you are being faithful to someone or something else. That something else is a weed. Pull it out!

2. Trust Him With Every Part of Your Life

3. Matthew 6:33

IV. Prepare to Hear - Having a Quiet Time / Preparing for Worship

A. Rest - Focus

B. Pray for Understanding

C. Seek to Hear What God Says to YOU

D. Determine to Obey

CPSIA information can be obtained
at www.ICGtesting.com
Printed in the USA
LVHW111521210921
698358LV00013B/160